HIT SONGS

T0039702

ISBN: 978-1-70519-879-7

Visit Hal Leonard Online at
www.halleonard.com

World headquarters, contact:
Hal Leonard
7777 West Bluemound Road
Milwaukee, WI 53213
Email: info@halleonard.com

In Europe, contact:
Hal Leonard Europe Limited
1 Red Place
London, W1K 6PL
Email: info@halleonardeurope.com

In Australia, contact:
Hal Leonard Australia Pty. Ltd.
4 Lentara Court
Cheltenham, Victoria, 3192 Australia
Email: info@halleonard.com.au

Easy on Me

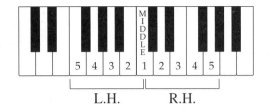

Words and Music by Adele Adkins
and Greg Kurstin

Moderate Ballad

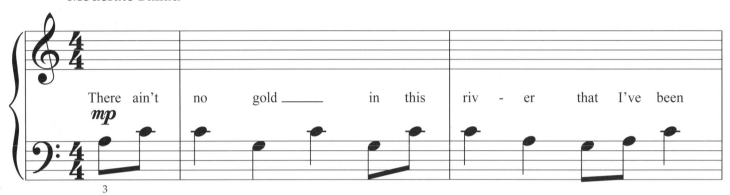

mp

There ain't no gold _____ in this riv - er that I've been

3

wash - ing my hands in for - ev - er. I know there is hope _____ in these

Duet Part (Student plays one octave higher than written.)

Moderate Ballad

p

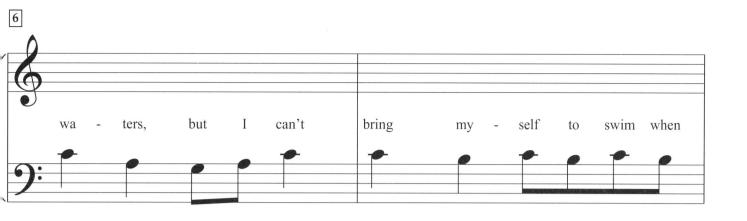

3

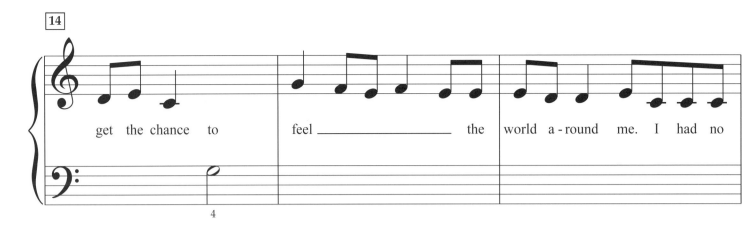

get the chance to feel _____ the world a-round me. I had no

time to choose _____ what I chose to do, so go eas - y on

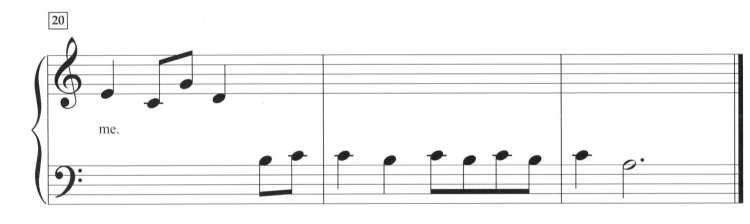

me.

4

Lift Me Up

from BLACK PANTHER: WAKANDA FOREVER

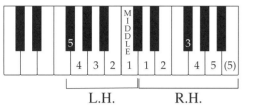

L.H.　　R.H.

Words and Music by Robyn Fenty,
Temilade Openiyi, Ludwig Göransson
and Ryan Coogler

With reverence

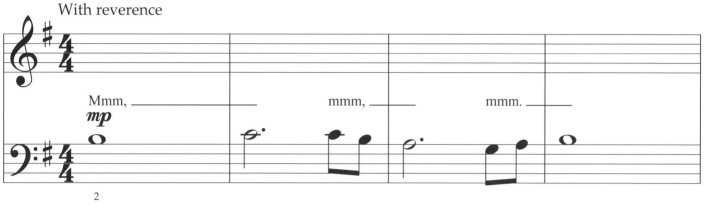

Mmm, _____　mmm, _____　mmm. _____

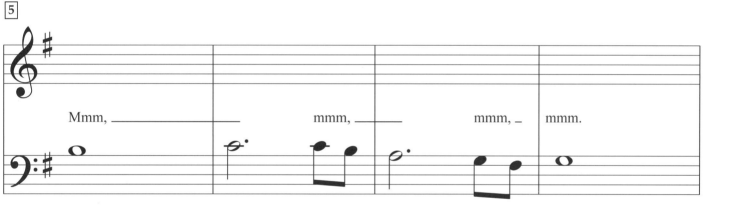

Mmm, _____　mmm, _____　mmm, _　mmm.

Duet Part (Student plays one octave higher than written.)

With reverence

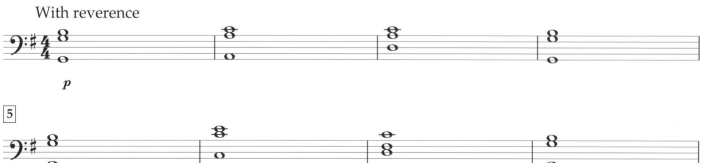

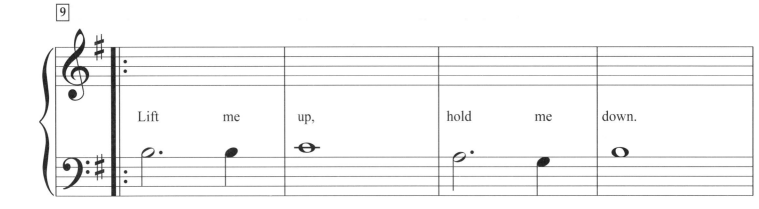

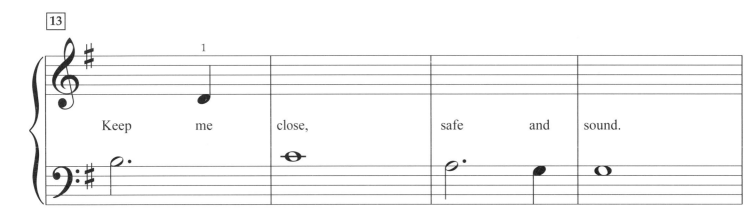

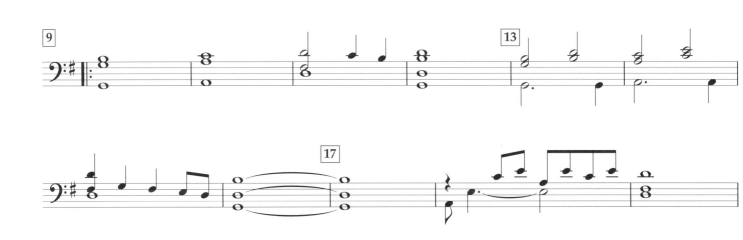

sleep. _____
me. _____
Keep me in the warmth of your
Keep me in the strength of your

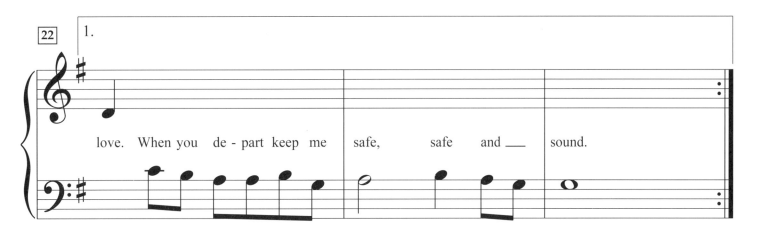

1.

love. When you de - part keep me safe, safe and ___ sound.

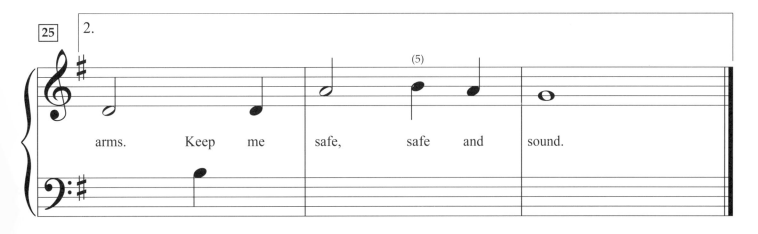

2.

arms. Keep me safe, safe and sound.

Flowers

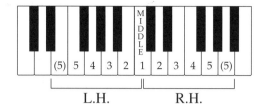

L.H.   R.H.

Words and Music by Miley Cyrus,
Gregory Hein and Michael Pollack

Disco Pop

mf
We were good, we were gold. Kind of dream that can't be

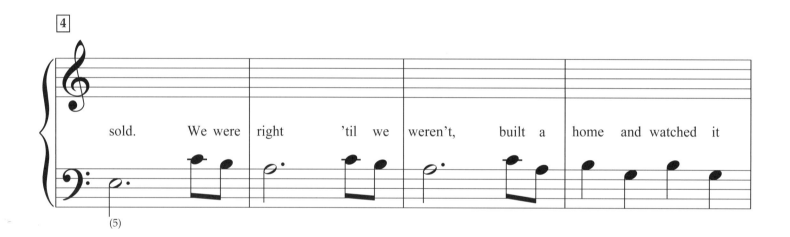

sold. We were right 'til we weren't, built a home and watched it

Duet Part (Student plays one octave higher than written.)

Disco Pop

burn. Mmm, I did-n't want to leave you, I did-n't want to lie.

Start-ed to cry but then re - mem - bered I... I can buy my-self flow-

ers, write my name in the sand.

Hold My Hand

from TOP GUN: MAVERICK

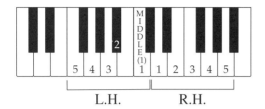

Words and Music by Stefani Germanotta
and Michael Tucker

Power Ballad

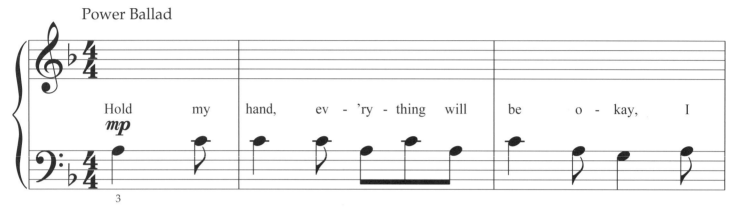

Hold my hand, ev-'ry-thing will be o-kay, I

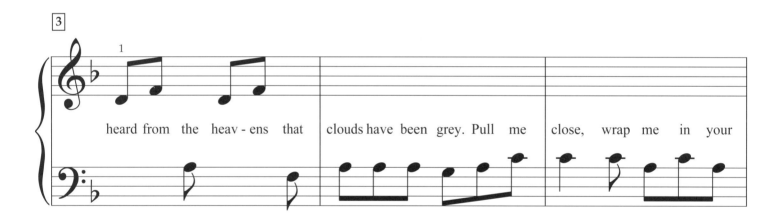

heard from the heav-ens that clouds have been grey. Pull me close, wrap me in your

Duet Part (Student plays one octave higher than written.)

Power Ballad

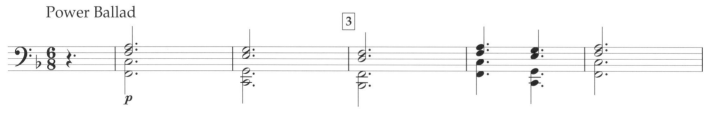

ach - ing arms.   I | see that you're hurt - ing. Why'd | you take so long to

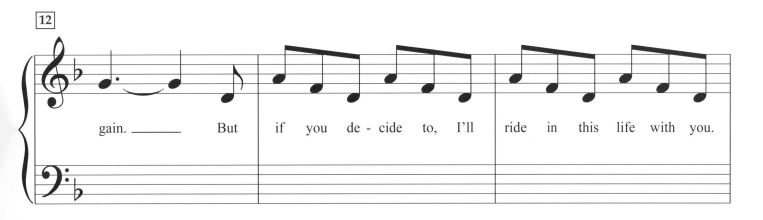

tell me you need me? I | see that you're bleed - ing. You | don't need to show me a -

gain. _____ But | if you de - cide to, I'll | ride in this life with you.

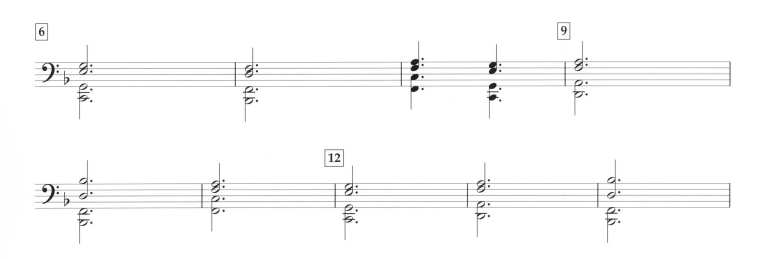

13

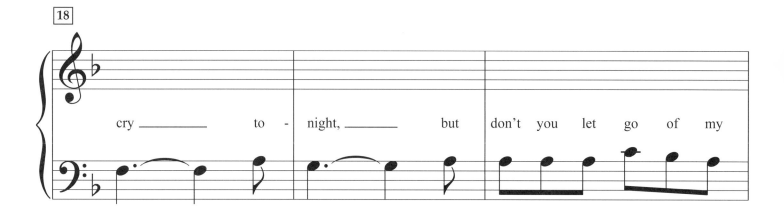

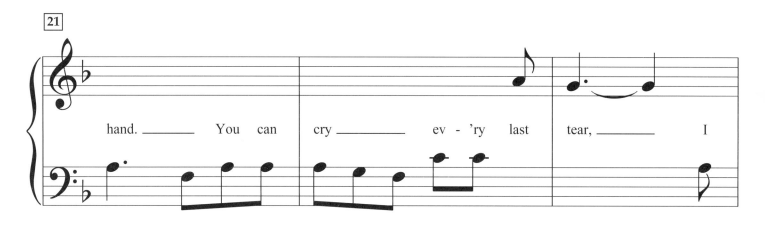

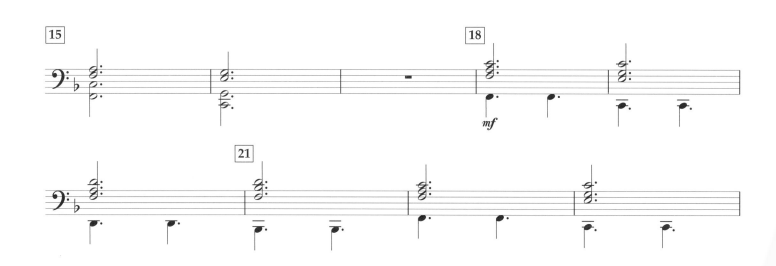

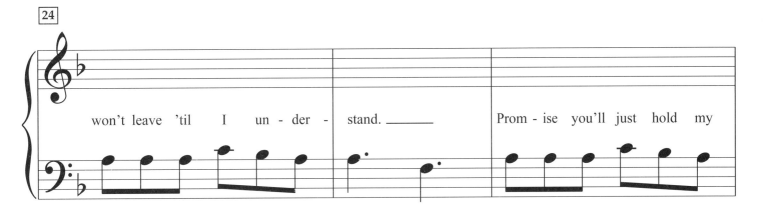

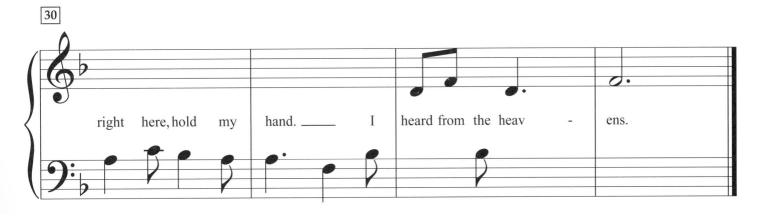

No Time to Die
from NO TIME TO DIE

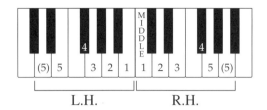

Words and Music by Billie Eilish O'Connell
and Finneas O'Connell

Moderately slow

I should have known ___ I'd leave a -
lone. Just goes to show ___ that the

Duet Part (Student plays one octave higher than written.)

Moderately slow

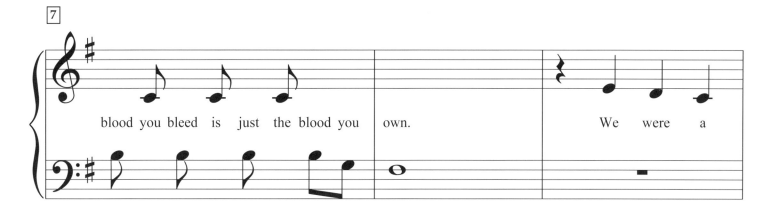

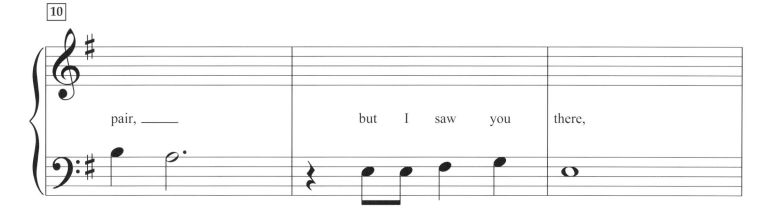

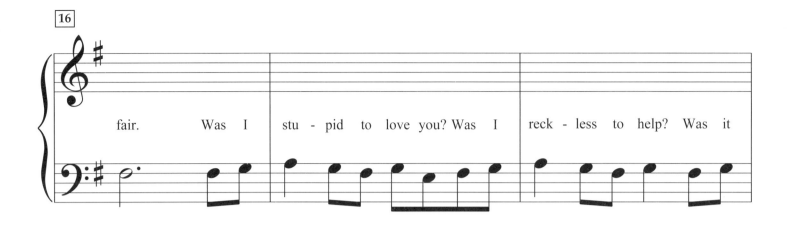

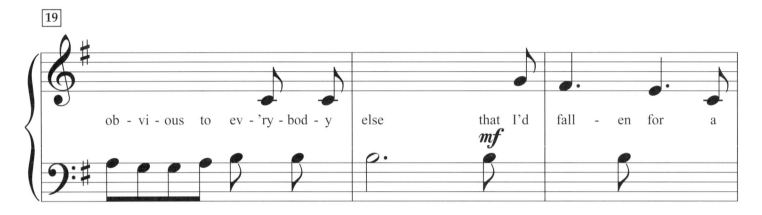

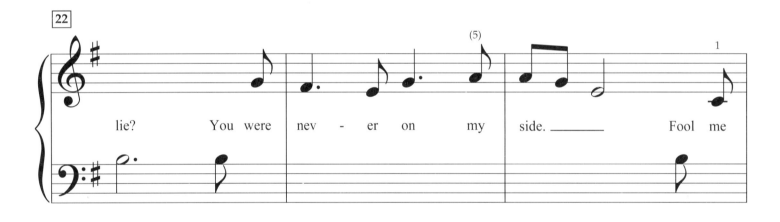

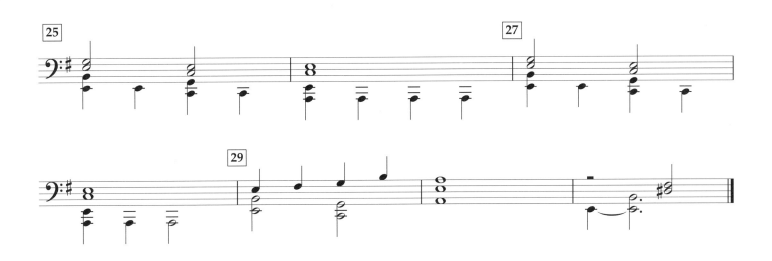

Shallow
from A STAR IS BORN

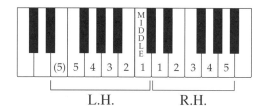

Words and Music by Stefani Germanotta,
Mark Ronson, Andrew Wyatt
and Anthony Rossomando

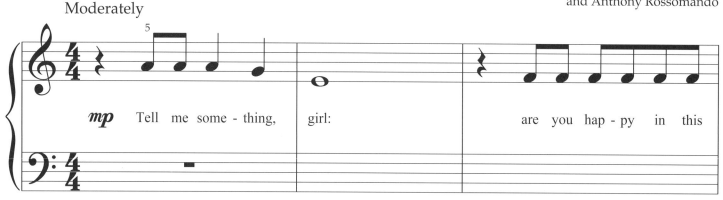

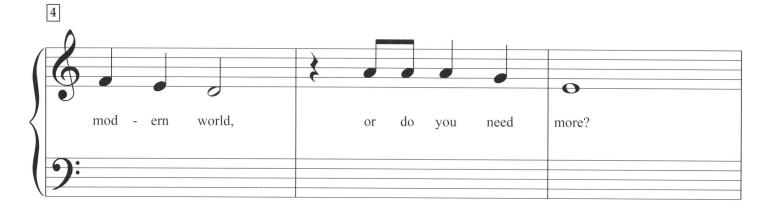

Duet Part (Student plays one octave higher than written.)

Moderately

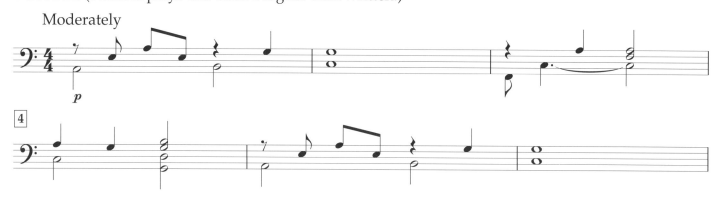

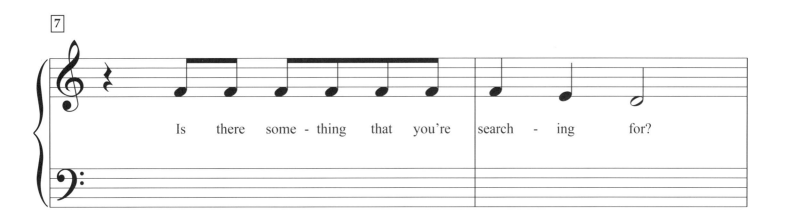

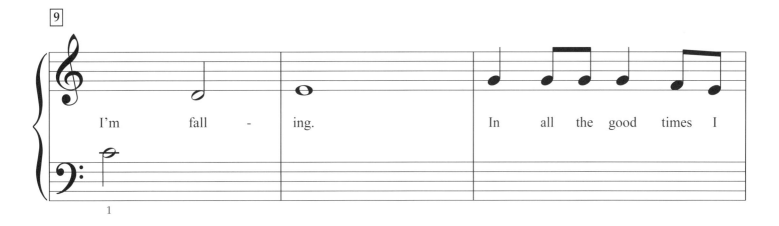

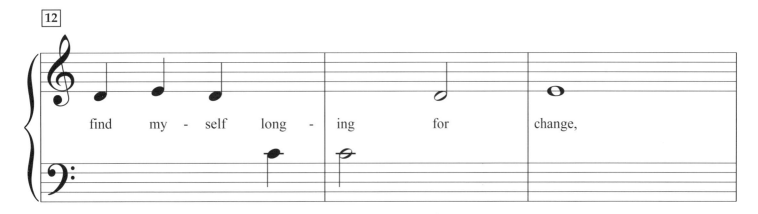

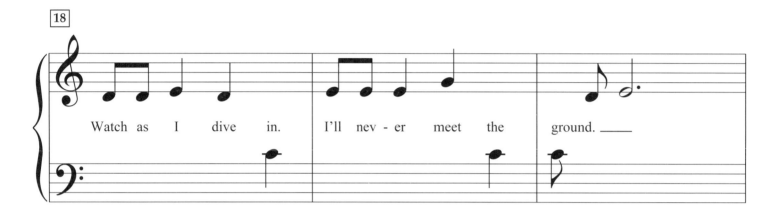

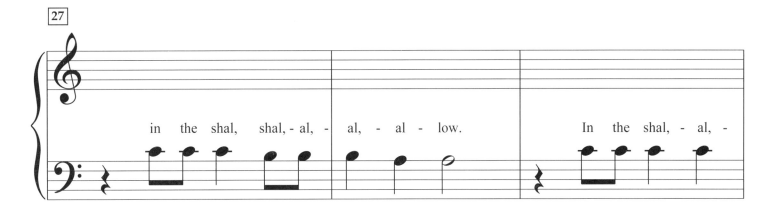

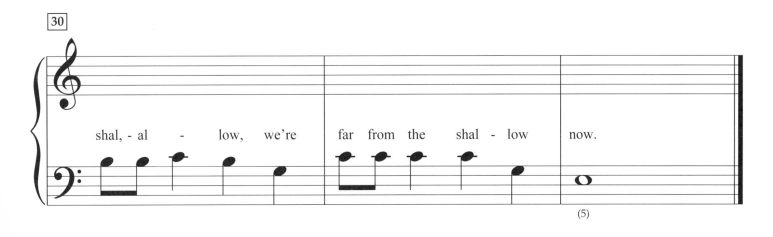

(5)

We Don't Talk About Bruno
from ENCANTO

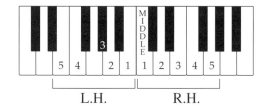

Music and Lyrics by
Lin-Manuel Miranda

Moderately

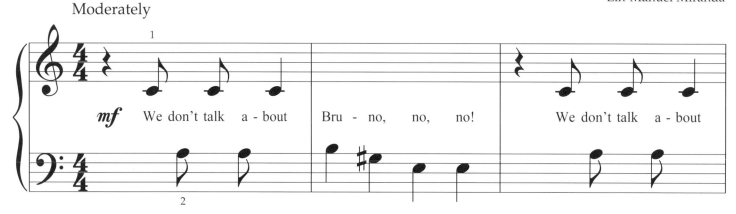

Duet Part (Student plays one octave higher than written.)

Moderately

was-n't a cloud in the sky. Bru - no walks in with a

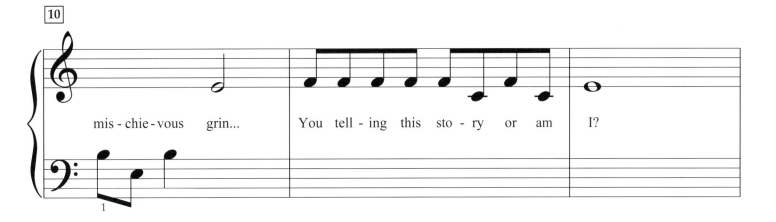

mis - chie - vous grin... You tell - ing this sto - ry or am I?

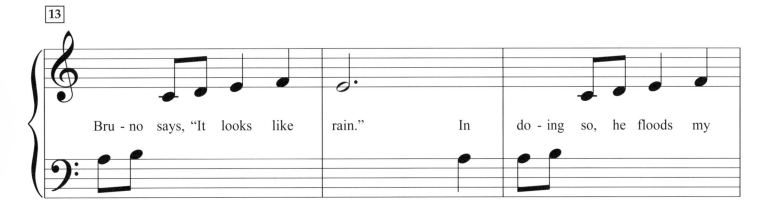

Bru - no says, "It looks like rain." In do - ing so, he floods my

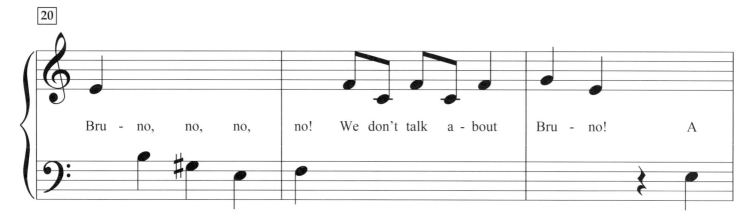

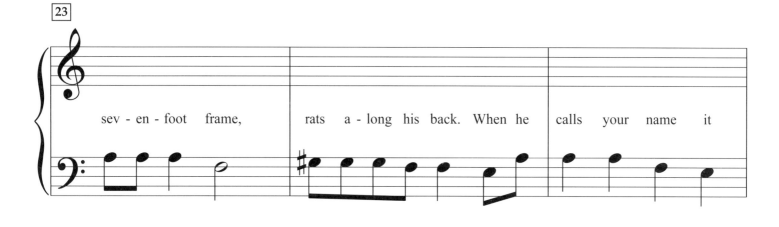

You Say

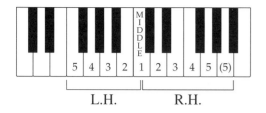

Words and Music by Lauren Daigle,
Bebo Norman, Paul Mabury,
Jason Ingram and Michael Donehey

I keep fight-ing voic-es in my mind that say I'm not e - nough,
Am I more than just the sum of ev - 'ry high and ev - 'ry low?

Re - ev - 'ry sin-gle lie that tells me I will nev - er meas - ure up.
mind me once a - gain just who I am, be-cause I need to know.

Duet Part (Student plays one octave higher than written.)

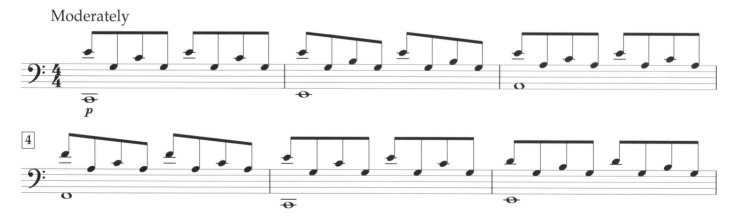

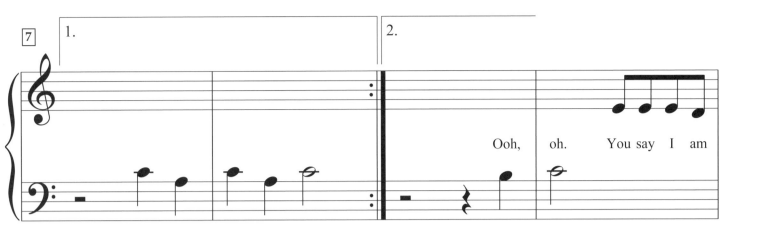

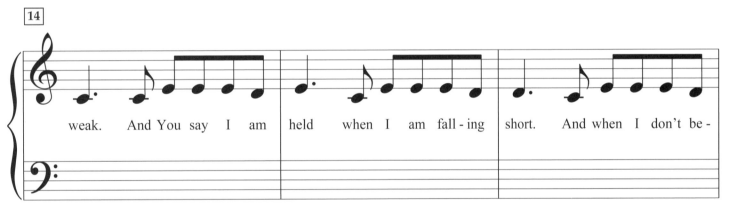

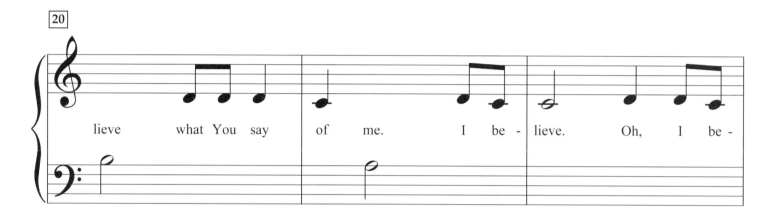

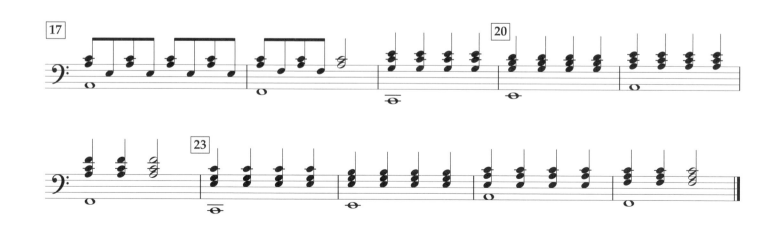

Enjoy Playing Great Hit Songs on Piano Now with Music from Your Favorite
CLASSIC & CONTEMPORARY ARTISTS

Order these and many more easy piano songbooks from Hal Leonard

ABBA – GOLD
00306820 19 songs $19.99

ADELE – 21
00307320 11 songs $22.99

ADELE – 25
00155394 11 songs $16.99

ADELE – 30
00396759 12 songs $22.99

THE BEATLES – 1
00307219 27 songs $22.99

THE BEATLES BEST
00231944 120 songs $27.99

THE BEATLES GREATEST HITS
00490364 25 songs $19.99

BEST OF JUSTIN BIEBER
00248635 12 songs $14.99

BEST OF MICHAEL BUBLÉ
00307144 14 songs $17.99

BEST OF CARPENTERS
00306427 18 songs $19.99

BEST OF CHICAGO
00306536 16 songs $19.99

ERIC CLAPTON COLLECTION
00277346 11 songs $19.99

BEST OF COLDPLAY
00306560 16 songs $19.99

BOB DYLAN
14041363 13 songs $16.99

EAGLES GREATEST HITS
00293339 10 songs $14.99

BILLIE EILISH – HAPPIER THAN EVER
00369298 15 songs $19.99

BILLIE EILISH – WHEN WE ALL FALL ASLEEP WHERE DO WE GO?
00323126 13 songs $19.99

BEST OF FLEETWOOD MAC
00109467 12 songs $19.99

ARIANA GRANDE
00293337 14 songs $19.99

IMAGINE DRAGONS
00294441 14 songs $19.99

MICHAEL JACKSON NUMBER ONES
00322301 18 songs $22.99

BILLY JOEL
00356295 21 songs $19.99

BEST OF BILLY JOEL
00110007 21 songs $19.99

ELTON JOHN ANTHOLOGY
00357102 30 songs $22.99

ELTON JOHN GREATEST HITS
00222538 17 songs $19.99

BEST OF NORAH JONES
00354465 14 songs $19.99

CAROLE KING – TAPESTRY
00306555 12 songs $19.99

BEST OF JOHN LEGEND
00224732 14 songs $19.99

THE LUMINEERS
00334067 15 songs $19.99

BOB MARLEY
00129927 14 songs $17.99

MAROON 5
00152665 13 songs $14.99

BEST OF BRUNO MARS
00221887 11 songs $19.99

MILEY CYRUS – ENDLESS SUMMER VACATON
01229481 12 songs $22.99

KACEY MUSGRAVES – GOLDEN HOUR
00350622 13 songs $19.99

KATY PERRY
00248632 12 songs $17.99

THE PIANO GUYS – SIMPLIFIED FAVORITES, VOL. 1
00127421 12 songs $19.99

THE PIANO GUYS – SIMPLIFIED FAVORITES, VOL. 2
00234609 14 songs $24.99

ELVIS PRESLEY – GREATEST HITS
00308205 27 songs $19.99

PRINCE – ULTIMATE
00302630 28 songs $24.99

QUEEN COLLECTION
00139187 10 songs $19.99

BEST OF ED SHEERAN
01052267 17 songs $19.99

SAM SMITH – THE THRILL OF IT ALL
00257747 14 songs $17.99

TAYLOR SWIFT – EVERMORE
00363715 17 songs $22.99

TAYLOR SWIFT – FEARLESS
00307060 13 songs $16.99

TAYLOR SWIFT – FOLKLORE
00356888 17 songs $24.99

TAYLOR SWIFT – LOVER
00322685 18 songs $19.99

TAYLOR SWIFT – MIDNIGHTS
01141779 13 songs $22.99

U2 – 18 SINGLES
00307285 18 songs $22.99

STEVIE WONDER ANTHOLOGY
00306258 27 songs $19.99

HAL•LEONARD®
www.halleonard.com
Prices, contents, and availability subject to change without notice.

PLAYING PIANO HAS NEVER BEEN EASIER!

Five-Finger Piano songbooks from Hal Leonard are designed for students in their first year of study. They feature single-note melody lines that stay in one position, indicated by a small keyboard diagram at the beginning of each song. Each song also includes lyrics, and beautifully written piano accompaniments that can be played by teachers, parents or more experienced students to give new players a "it sounds so good!" experience.

 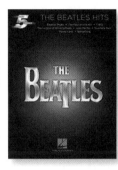    

Adele
00175097   8 songs $9.99

Beatles! Beatles!
00292061   8 songs $8.99

Beatles Favorites
00310369   8 songs $10.99

The Beatles Hits
00128687   8 songs $8.99

Cartoon Fun
00279151   8 songs $8.99

A Charlie Brown Christmas™
00316069   10 songs $12.99

The Charlie Brown Collection™
00316072   8 songs $8.99

Children's TV Favorites
00311208   8 songs $7.95

Christmas Carols
00236800   10 songs $8.99

Christmas Songs Made Easy
00172307   10 songs $10.99

Church Songs for Kids
00310613   15 songs $9.99

Classical Favorites
00310611   12 selections...................... $8.99

Classical Themes
00310469   10 songs $7.95

Disney Classics
00311429   7 songs $8.99

Disney Delights
00310195   9 songs $8.99

Disney Favorites
00311038   8 songs $10.99

Disney Latest Movie Hits
00277255   8 songs $10.99

Disney Movie Classics
00123475   8 songs $10.99

Disney Songs
00283429   8 songs $9.99

Disney Today
00175218   8 songs $10.99

Disney Tunes
00310375   8 songs $9.99

Disney's Princess Collection
00310847   7 songs $12.99

Eensy Weensy Spider & Other Nursery Rhyme Favorites
00310465   11 songs $7.95

Favorite Christmas Songs
00367574   10 songs............................ $9.99

First Pop Songs
00123296   8 songs $9.99

Frozen
00130374   7 songs $14.99

Frozen 2
00329705   8 songs $16.99

Fun Songs
00346769   8 songs $8.99

Hallelujah and Other Songs of Inspiration
00119649   9 songs $7.99

Happy Birthday to You and Other Great Songs
00102097   10 songs $7.99

Irish Songs
00312078   9 songs $6.99

The Lion King
00292062   5 songs $12.99

Modern Movie Favorites
00242674   8 songs $10.99

Movie Hits
00338187   8 songs $9.99

My First Hymn Book
00311873   12 songs $9.99

Over the Rainbow and Other Great Songs
00102098   10 songs $7.99

Pirates of the Caribbean
00123473   8 songs $14.99

Pop Hits
00123295   8 songs $9.99

Praise & Worship
00311044   8 songs $7.95

The Sound of Music
00310249   8 songs $12.99

Star Wars
00322185   10 songs $12.99

Star Wars: A Musical Journey
00322311   15 songs $16.99

Star Wars: Selections
00321903   9 songs $12.99

Today's Hits
00277909   8 songs $9.99

The Very Best of Broadway
00311039   8 songs $7.95

HAL•LEONARD®

View songlists and order online from your favorite music retailer at
halleonard.com